DEVELOPMENTAL READING ASSESSMENT
RESOURCE GUIDE

By Joetta Beaver

*in Collaboration with
Primary Classroom Teachers*

Celebration Press
An Imprint of Pearson Learning

Acknowledgments

The creation and ongoing refinement of the Developmental Reading Assessment for primary students is the result of much collaboration with many teachers. Without their help and enthusiasm, the DRA would not have come to pass. Many thanks to:

Cheri Slinger for all her insights, expertise, and help throughout the process.

Kathleen Taps and **Amy Mayr** for formatting the DRA forms.

John Heck for the photographs and videotapes.

Mark Carter for listening and sharing his insights over the years.

Kathy Collins for formatting the DRA Continuum

Homer Mincy and **John Sonedecker** for backing innovative projects and trusting the process.

William Schaefer and **Bob O'Brien** for their continued support of the process.

Gay Su Pinnell, Carol Lyons, Diane DeFord, and **Andrea McCarrier** for fostering and supporting teachers as learners.

Jane Williams for her leadership in field-testing the DRA.

Cheryl Seelbach for her typing and retyping and retyping.

The following primary teachers, who worked during the summer, used the DRA materials and procedures with their students and gave good feedback and suggestions over the years:

Paula Samansky

Jean Sperling

Carolyn Carleton

Peggy Glenn

Linda Gordon

Patty Nichols

Barbara Spitzer

Kathy Havens

Ann Patrick

Janet Barry

Marsha McAtee

Sabrina DeLibera

Sue Bauchmoyer

Jennifer MacNaughton

Debbie Houser

Sherlyn Porter

Sarah Schriner

Tamar Sorin

Terry Trubiano

Jo Reece

Jenesse Wells

Peggy DeLapp

Sue Reed

Carrie Keener

Karen Boreman

Sandy Miller

Chic Allison

Mary Clark Smith

Annette Hegemier

Table of Contents

Introduction

The number one goal of any reading program should be to help students become proficient, enthusiastic readers who enjoy reading and read for a variety of purposes. This Developmental Reading Assessment (DRA) can help teachers achieve this goal by providing a method for assessing and documenting primary students' development as readers over time within a literature-based instructional reading program. The DRA is designed to be used in kindergarten through third-grade classrooms with rich literate environments. In such classrooms, reading and writing are taught as reciprocal processes, a wide variety of children's books is available and accessible, and reading and writing activities fulfill meaningful purposes. On a daily basis, all students

*   hear a variety of literature read aloud

*   read independently for a sustained period of time

*   respond to literature in a variety of ways

*   receive instruction and support in guided-reading groups and/or individual reading conferences

Developmental Reading Assessments are conducted during one-on-one reading conferences as children read specially selected assessment texts. *Developmental Reading Assessment* describes DRA procedures for primary students and provides assessment texts, a teacher's resource book, and assessment masters designed to help assess students during these conferences. The procedures incorporate the exemplary work of Dr. Marie M. Clay of New Zealand, including the use of running records described by her in *An Observation Survey of Early Literacy Achievement* (Heinemann 1993) to record and analyze observable reading behaviors.

The DRA was developed, field-tested, and revised by primary teachers in the Upper Arlington City School District in Ohio between 1988 and 1996. Procedures, forms, and assessment texts have changed over the years in response to teachers' feedback and suggestions. The goal of all revisions has been to create an effective, informative, and practical reading assessment for primary students.

In May 1996, seventy-eight primary classroom and Reading Recovery teachers from urban, suburban, rural, and small-town school districts from different regions of the United States and twenty-two teachers in Canada field-tested the DRA. Eighty-four of these teachers returned feedback forms. As a group, they conducted 295 DRA conferences with primary students. The results indicated the teachers' overall satisfaction with the DRA.

Further revisions to the observation forms and assessment texts were made during the summer of 1996 based on feedback and suggestions from the May field-testing. In October of that year, Upper Arlington primary classroom and Reading Recovery teachers conducted approximately 250 DRA conferences using the latest forms and assessment texts. They were very satisfied with the assessment.

Even though primary teachers in the Upper Arlington City Schools and those who participated in the field-testing were very satisfied with the DRA, you may find it necessary to modify the DRA procedures, observation forms, levels of proficiency, or continuum to fit your particular needs. In that case, make changes as needed, but please honor and give credit for original work.

The DRA can be used on an annual, semi-annual, or quarterly basis to document change over time in each student's reading. It also allows you to look forward and plan for future learning. Indeed, the teachers who have worked over the years to create the DRA hope that it enables primary teachers to observe, record, and evaluate changes in students' performance as readers and to plan for and teach what each student needs to learn next.

Teachers must help primary students to become good readers. To do so, they must recognize the characteristics and behaviors of good readers and foster them in their students.

Good readers select appropriately leveled reading materials and continue to improve as readers each time they read.

Students' ability to select appropriate reading materials is a critical factor in their reading development, especially within a literature-based reading program.

As part of the DRA, students reading at end-of-first-grade levels and above select from a range of three or four texts chosen by the teacher one that is just right for them — not too easy and not too hard.

Good readers read and sustain their reading for longer periods of time.

Their ability to read increases as they spend time reading appropriately leveled texts. Helping students engage and sustain their own reading is an essential part of a primary reading program. This ability develops and changes over time.

The DRA suggests that teachers note the level of support needed by students for reading familiar texts, new texts, and new genres.

Good readers read aloud quickly and smoothly.

They phrase generously and meaningfully, possibly pausing just slightly at difficulty, and they use effective intonation and stress to construct meaning. Helping primary students learn to read fluently in long, meaningful phrases with appropriate intonation is essential for good comprehension and ease in reading extended stories.

As part of the DRA, teachers note and monitor changes over time in students' pace, phrasing, expression, and attention to punctuation as they read orally.

Good readers preview a book or story before reading it and can predict what might happen.

They know that doing so actually makes the reading easier. Good readers read the information on the book jacket, leaf through the book quickly to get a feel for the layout, and read a little bit here and there before settling down with the book. The information gathered from the preview, along with prior knowledge, enables readers to predict what might happen. It would be impossible for a teacher to introduce every book a student might read, nor would it be in the student's best interest. It is important that students learn how to preview a text for themselves and how to use the information they gain from previewing to facilitate reading.

The DRA assesses students' ability to preview text and predict what might happen.

Good readers use a variety of strategies.

They detect and correct errors and problem-solve unknown words flexibly and automatically while reading.

During the DRA, teachers note reading behaviors such as pausing, rereading, searching the pictures, appealing for help, sounding out clusters of letters, self-correcting, and so on as evidence of students' use of various strategies.

Good readers read for meaning.

When meaning breaks down, they take some action to reconstruct it as they read. They relate what they read to their own background knowledge, personal experiences, and other literature. They are aware of implied meanings. They think about and evaluate what they read. When children are asked to retell, respond to, and extend the stories they read, they realize that understanding what one reads is important.

To assess students' level of comprehension, they are asked to retell the story they have just read and respond to questions during the DRA conference. To discover what students remember about a story often requires prompting and further questioning.

Good readers read and function within a literacy community.

They have favorite books, authors, and possibly genres. They enjoy reading. They find the time to read and generally have preferences about where, when, and with whom they read. They tell others about what they are reading and read books recommended by others. They participate in book groups, as well as share what they have learned from reading. Helping students become members of a literacy community begins in kindergarten, if not before.

The questions about reading preferences on the DRA help teachers become aware of students' preferences and alert them when students grow passive about reading.

The above observations of good readers and the reading process are supported and described in greater depth and detail by Marie Clay in *Becoming Literate: The Construction of Inner Control*; Don Holdaway in *The Foundations of Literacy* and *Independence in Reading*; and Frank Smith in *Understanding Reading* and *Joining the Literacy Club*.

Developmental Reading Assessment Texts

The DRA assessment texts represent a range of text difficulty. The following factors were used to select and determine levels of difficulty: language and story structures; story appeal, concepts, vocabulary, and experiences common to a majority of primary children; level of picture support; and text size, layout, and number of words. Levels of text difficulty are indicated on a scale from A through 44.

Levels A–2

Assessment texts A through 2 consist of a repeated word or sentence pattern with natural language structures. The simple illustrations include animals and objects familiar to primary children and highly support the text. One or two lines of text appear on the left page and are large and well spaced so that children can point as they read. The number of words in the texts ranges from ten to thirty-six.

The train can go.

Levels 3–8

Assessment texts 3 through 8 comprise simple stories that contain repetitive words, phrases, and actions. They use mostly predictable language structures. The stories include characters and experiences that are familiar to primary children, and pictures still provide much support. One to three lines of text are generally placed below the picture. The number of words in the texts ranges from forty-six to eighty-six.

Jim had a dog. The dog was black and white. The dog's name was Duke.

2

Duke was a big dog. He had big feet. Jim liked his dog.

3

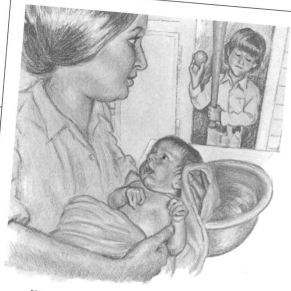

Mama was giving Maria a bath.
So Mama was too busy to play with
Robert. Robert felt left out. Mama was
taking care of his baby sister.

6

Papa was feeding Maria.
So Papa was too busy to read to
Robert. Robert felt left out. Papa was
taking care of his baby sister.

7

Levels 10–14

Assessment texts 10 through 14 are stories that begin to introduce problems and solutions. The stories are about children and problems to which children can relate. There is some repetition of events in each of the stories. Book and oral language structures are incorporated and the number of high-frequency words is expanded. The illustrations give moderate support, provide information about the setting, and suggest the sequence of events. The text, consisting of two to five lines, is located under the illustrations. The number of words in the texts ranges from 129 to 203.

A chipmunk came skipping along. The chipmunk stopped at the pond. She looked at herself in the water, and she smiled. Then she patted her golden-brown fur with her paw.

"My fur looks pretty today, doesn't it?" said the chipmunk.

"Yes," said Freddie the Frog. "It looks very pretty."

"Don't you wish you looked like me?" asked the chipmunk.

"No," said Freddie the Frog. "I look OK."

"But look at you," said the chipmunk. "You poor thing. You're all green."

Then the chipmunk skipped away, all shining and golden brown in the sunshine.

Freddie the Frog sat on his log. He wasn't eating. He wasn't drinking. He wasn't thinking. He was crying.

The wise old owl came flying by. He stopped at the pond. He looked at Freddie the Frog. "Why are you crying, Freddie?" asked the owl. "It's such a pretty day. No one should be crying on such a pretty day."

Levels 16–28

Assessment texts 16 through 28 are stories with beginnings, middles, and ends, throughout which problems are presented and resolved. The characters are either imaginary (giants and elves) or animals with human characteristics. The content begins to move beyond children's personal experiences and builds a basis with which to compare and contrast other stories. Literary language structures are integrated with natural language. Some description of characters and setting is included. Illustrations provide moderate to minimum support. The text may be three to twelve lines above or beneath the illustrations, or a full page. The number of words in these texts starts at 266 and increases with each level of difficulty.

Levels 30–44

Assessment texts 30 through 44 are more complex stories that describe the setting, characters, problem(s), and resolution(s) in more detail. More sophisticated language structures and challenging vocabulary are incorporated. This group of stories presents three different genres — realistic fiction, folk tale, and animal adventure. Background knowledge and higher-level thinking skills are needed to understand and appreciate the humor, the problem, or the suspense in each story. There is a minimum of picture support. Text size is slightly smaller and fills full pages or partial pages with illustrations.

Big Les and Lester, his son, lived in No-End Hollow and raised foxhounds for a living. Their dogs were the finest hounds in all that part of Tennessee. People came from North Carolina, Georgia, and Alabama to buy foxhounds from them.

Now Lester had a pet hound that was not for sale to anybody. Funny Face was his name—Funny for short. Lester had been offered as high as fifty dollars for Funny, and that was a mighty big price at that time. But Lester loved Funny too much to sell him to anybody.

Funny followed Lester everywhere he went. That fall when school started, the teacher made a rule that said all dogs had to be left at home. It nearly broke Funny's heart to be left behind. Lester hated to leave him, but there was nothing else to do. As Lester was on his way to school one morning, he heard a familiar bark. Funny was racing after him. Lester felt so sorry for the dog that he hadn't the heart to scold him. He petted him for a minute or two. Then he said, "I'll have to take you home again even if it makes me late to school."

As they were going up the hollow, they had to pass right by Old Ben Bailey's place. He was standing by his front gate, and when he saw them, he understood what had happened.

"Too bad about your dog running away," he said. "Now you'll be late for school and you'll likely get a whipping for that. But I have a fine notion, Lester. Leave your dog here with me and pick him up on your way home this afternoon."

2

3

✳At the heart of the DRA is the one-on-one conference. Such conferences permit you to observe and interact with students, recording their responses and behaviors as they read and respond to the texts read. The information gathered will enable you to

- determine a reader's independent assessment reading level

- confirm or redirect ongoing instruction

- group students effectively for reading experiences and instruction

- document changes over time in reading performance

- identify students who may be working below proficiency and need further assessments Pg 39 Wh to do.

The format for the DRA conference changes over time to honor what readers can do as they move toward independence. What students are asked to do during the DRA changes so that teachers may support readers at different stages of development.

Students Reading DRA Levels A, 1, 2

For students reading assessment text levels A through 2, the teacher selects the appropriate assessment text and then reads one or two pages of the text to introduce the text pattern before asking students to read. He or she takes a running record as they read and records observations on the appropriate DRA observation guide. The reading preference questions ask for information about who reads to them and what story they like to hear.

The assessment texts for these readers are:

A *Can You Sing?*

1 *Things That Go*

2 *I Can See*

Students Reading DRA Levels 3–16

For students reading assessment text levels 3 through 16, the teacher introduces the selected text and then listens as they tell what is happening in the illustrations to see if the students gather pertinent information and begin to construct a story prior to reading the story aloud. He or she takes a running record as they read and records observations on the DRA observation guide for the selected text. After reading aloud, the children retell the story. The teacher may ask them to tell more if the initial retelling is incomplete or may ask other questions if she or he feels students know more about the story than indicated by the retelling. The reading preference questions ask who reads to or with them, what story they like to hear, and whether they like to read.

The assessment texts for these readers are:

3 *The "I Like" Game*

4 *Where Is My Hat?*

6 *Why Are We Stopping?*

8 *Duke*

10 *Shoe Boxes*

12 *Robert's New Friend*

14 *The Wagon*

16 *The Pot of Gold*

Students Reading DRA Levels 18–44

For students reading assessment text levels 18 through 44, the teacher asks the students to select an assessment text that is just right from a range of three or four choices. The teacher introduces the text selected and has students read the beginning paragraphs aloud. If the selection seems to be at an appropriate level, she or he asks readers to predict what they think might happen in the story and then has them read the complete story independently at their seats or somewhere else in the classroom. After students read the complete story silently, they retell the story, respond to specific questions, and then read aloud a selected portion of the text.

The teacher takes a running record of each student's oral reading and records observations on the DRA observation guide for the selected text.

The reading preference questions for students reading levels 18-24 ask for information about their favorite book, where and when they like to read, and if they like to read alone, with a buddy, or with a group. Readers at level 28 and above are asked why they read, who is their favorite author, and why they chose the book they're presently reading.

The assessment texts for these readers are:

18 *A Giant in the Forest*

20 *Green Freddie*

24 *The Wonderful Day*

28 *You Don't Look Beautiful to Me*

30 *Touchdown!*

34 *Be Nice to Josephine*

38 *Trouble at the Beaver Pond*

40 *Old Ben Bailey Meets His Match*

44 *Danger in the Deep*

LOCATOR GUIDE

The following guide lists several books that are comparable to the DRA text levels and their approximate grade levels. These books were sorted by common characteristics and leveled by classroom teachers. It is hoped that this list of books will enable teachers to select an appropriate DRA text. Thinking about where and what a student is reading on a daily basis and locating similar books on the guide should give the teacher a general sense of which book(s) to select for the DRA conference. After the conference the teacher may use the guide once again to think about what types and levels of books the student is ready to read next.

In Chapter 6 of *Bridges to Literacy*, Barbara Peterson presents an overview of the characteristics of books leveled by difficulty for beginning readers. Levels for guided reading books for students in kindergarten through third grade are described by Irene Fountas and Gay Su Pinnell in *Guided Reading: Good First Teaching for All Children*. Both resources include lists of leveled books and discuss how to use the information in selecting books that are appropriate for readers at various stages of development.

Grade Level / DRA Texts	*Comparable Book Titles*
Kindergarten	
A *Can You Sing?*	*Colors* (Anderson/Dutton)
1 *Things That Go*	*My Book* (Maris/Viking)
2 *I Can See*	*So Can I* (Facklam/Harcourt Brace)
Preprimer	
3 *The "I Like" Game*	*Baby Says* (Steptoe/Morrow)
4 *Where Is My Hat?*	*Brown Bear, Brown Bear* (Martin/Holt)
6 *Why Are We Stopping?*	*How Many Bugs in a Box?* (Carter/Simon & Schuster)
8 *Duke*	*Go, Dog, Go!* (Eastman/Random House)
Primer	
10 *Shoe Boxes*	*Just Like Daddy* (Asch/Simon & Schuster) *Cookies Week* (Ward/Puttman)
12 *Robert's New Friend*	*Gone Fishing* (Long/Houghton Mifflin) *Titch* (Hutchins/Penguin)

Grade Level / DRA Texts	Comparable Book Titles

First Grade

14 *The Wagon*

Clean House for Mole and Mouse (Ziefert/Scholastic)
Fix-It (McPhail/Penguin)

16 *The Pot of Gold*
(K stop)

Are You My Mother? (Eastman/Random House)
Just Me and My Dad (Mayer/Donovon)

Second Grade

18 *A Giant in the Forest*

Little Bear (Minarik/ Harper Collins)
Frog and Toad (Lobel/Harper & Rowe)

20 *Green Freddie*

Henry and Mudge (Rylant/Aladdin)
Fox All Week (Marshall/Dial Books)

24 *The Wonderful Day*

Arthur books (Hoban/Harper Collins)
Nate the Great (Weinman/Dell)

28 *You Don't Look Beautiful to Me*
(1st grade stop)

All About Stacy (Giff/Dell)
The Stories Julian Tells (Cameron/Random House)

Third Grade

30 *Touchdown!*

Cam Jansen (Adler/Puffin Books)
Peewee Scouts series (Delton/Dell)

34 *Be Nice to Josephine*

Zombies Don't Play Soccer (Dadey and Jones/Scholastic)
The Hit Away Kid (Christopher/Dell)
Freckle Juice (Blume/Dell Yearling)

38 *Trouble at the Beaver Pond*
(2nd grade stop)

Shark in School (Giff/Dell)
Box Car Children (Warner/Albert Whitman)

Fourth Grade

40 *Old Ben Bailey Meets His Match*

Chocolate Fever (Smith/Yearling)
Runaway Ralph books (Cleary/Avon)
Little House on the Prairie (Wilder/Harper & Rowe)

Fifth Grade

44 *Danger in the Deep*

Matilda (Dahl/Puffin)
Encyclopedia Brown books (Sobel/Bantam)

This resource includes a number of forms for assessing students' reading and recording their progress over time.

Observation Guides

The observation guides include teacher directions, questions, and prompts for the assessment texts. The teacher records his or her observations of the student's reading behaviors and responses in the designated spaces. An observation guide has been designed for each assessment text.

Date 3/97

Name Chris _____   Grade 1   Teacher _____

INTRODUCTION TO THE TEXT: PREVIEWING AND PREDICTING

T: Read the title and then say: *Kevin's two brothers and his sister used the same wagon for different things. Look at the pictures and tell me what is happening in this story.*

As the student previewed the pictures he/she gathered: ___ little ✓ some ___ pertinent information

___ commented on each picture as a separate event ✓ began to connect events ___ constructed a tentative story

T: Read the title again and then say: *Now read to find out how Kevin's brothers and sister fixed the dented, dirty wagon when it was his turn to have it.*

ORAL READING AND STRATEGIES USED

Take a running record as student reads.
Circle accuracy rate: Word Count 203

%	100	99	98	97	96	95	94	93	92	91	90	89
Miscues	0	1–3	4–5	6–7	8–9	10–11	12–13	14–15	16–17	18–19	20–21	22–23

(98 circled)

Phrasing and fluency: some   generally

Read: ✓ word by word   ✓ in short phrases   ___ in longer phrases   ___ punctuation

Reread for: ✓ phrasing   ___ punctuation

Intonation: ___ emerging   ✓ developing   ___ g...

Reading rate: ___ slow   ___ inconsistent   ✓ adeq...

At difficulty student:

Problem-solved by: ✓ picture   ✓ rereading   ✓...

___ multiple attempts   ✓ pa...

Appealed for help: ___ often   ___ sometimes

Number of words told/given by teacher: 0

Analysis of miscues:

Miscues interfered with meaning: ✓ yes

Self-corrected miscues that: ✓ didn't make sens...

Comments: Made few errors.
errors using meaning. O...
but neglected meaning.

COMPREHENSION AND RESPONSE

Close the book before the retelling and then say:
T: *Tell me in your own words what happened in the story.*

Initial retelling included: ✓ characters   ___ important details

___ setting   ___ events in sequence   ✓ some events out of sequence   ___ vocabulary/special phrases from story   ___ ending *thought it was Kev

wagon and he let the others use it and they gave it back all dirty

If initial retelling is incomplete, prompt:
T: *Tell me more.*

Added information about: ___ characters   ✓ important details

___ setting   ___ events   ___ ending   told what sister & brother did with the wagon

Use these questions only if the following information was omitted from retelling:

T: *Who used the wagon, and what did they use it for?*

T: *What happened when it was Kevin's turn to have the wagon?* they painted it and did all good stuff to it

Record other questions asked: ① What did Kevin think about the wagon? He liked it because it had his name on it.

Response:

T: *Did you like this story? Why or why not?* yes because it's about a wagon and my brother has a wagon.

T: *What does this story make you think of?* He got it for his birthday. ① What does he do with his wagon? plays with it; rides in it

Student's responses required: ___ restating questions   ✓ other questions   ✓ prompts   ___ no prompts

READING PREFERENCES

T: *Do you like to read* ✓ alone   ___ with a buddy   ___ with a group? *Why?* because if the other person messes up, we have to start over.

T: *When do you like to read? Why?* at school. We get to read different books.

T: *Where do you like to read? Why?* on the couch. It's fun.

T: *What is one of your favorite books? Why?* Cookie's Week. She gets into a lot trouble. ① What part do you like best? when she knocks down the curtain.

Circle the statements on the Developmental Reading Continuum that describe the student's performance.

Developmental Reading Assessment Continuum K–3

The DRA continuum enables the teacher to document each reader's development over time. A series of statements reflects a range of possible behaviors and responses across the emergent, early, transitional, and extending stages. Using the information recorded on the observation guide, teachers circle the statements that best describe the student's behaviors in the following areas: book selection and self-sustained reading, previewing and predicting, oral reading and use of strategies, and comprehension. Teachers will circle statements across stages because students do not develop as readers at the same rate or in the same way. Even students who are reading the same assessment text vary in their performance and responses.

The DRA continuum also gives teachers a scale for assessing a student's comprehension through retelling. However, comprehension is not correlated with each stage of development since it can vary within and across text levels. A teacher may decide that a reader's retelling reflects very little, some, an adequate, or a very good understanding at any text level. A student's prior experience with the genre or with retellings may have an effect on his or her level of comprehension. However, it's highly unlikely that an early reader's — or even a transitional reader's — retelling will reflect a very good understanding of the story, due to his or her stage of development and the type of texts he or she can read. It is equally unlikely that an extending reader's retelling would ever reflect very little understanding.

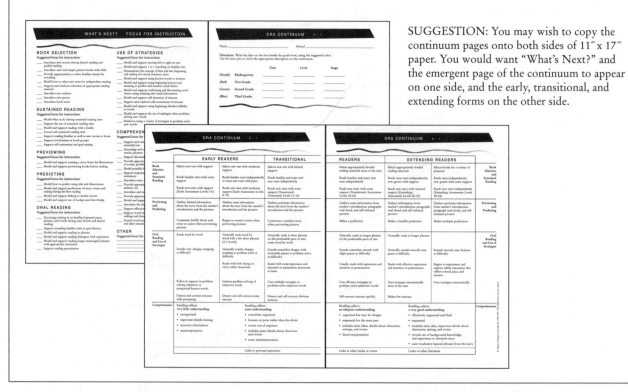

SUGGESTION: You may wish to copy the continuum pages onto both sides of 11″ x 17″ paper. You would want "What's Next?" and the emergent page of the continuum to appear on one side, and the early, transitional, and extending forms on the other side.

DRA CONTINUUM K–3

Name _Chris_   School _____

Directions: Write the date on the line beside the grade level, using the suggested color.
Use the same pen to circle the appropriate descriptors on the continuum.

		Date	Level	Stage
(Purple)	Kindergarten:	May '95	2	emergent
(Red)	First Grade:	March '96	14	transitional
(Green)	Second Grade:	___	___	
(Blue)	Third Grade:	___	___	

EMERGENT READERS

Book Selection	Requires others to select, read and/or share books	Relies on others to select text
	Relies on others to read text	(Reads familiar text with support)
		(Reads new texts with much support (Emergent Reader Assessment Levels A to 2))
Observable Reading Behaviors	Repeats a pattern without attending to the print	Moves left to right on one to three lines of text
	Points to words without matching one to one	(Matches one to one)
		(Locates and uses known words to monitor if she/he is right)
		(Differentiates words and letters)
	Invents the story	(Reads patterned text, using picture and oral language cues)

Developmental Reading Assessment Forms

After circling the selected statements on the continuum, the teacher identifies the stage that best reflects the student's performance. Using a different pen color to circle the statements for each grade level helps reflect the changes in the student's reading performance across the primary years.

Solid circles reflect observations in kindergarten.
Dashed circles reflect observations in first grade.

DRA CONTINUUM K–3

	EARLY READERS		TRANSITIONAL
Book Selection and Sustained Reading	Selects new text with support Reads familiar texts with some support Reads new texts with support (Early Assessment Levels 3-6)	Selects new text with moderate support Reads familiar texts independently or some new texts with peers Reads new texts with moderate support (Early Assessment Levels 8–10)	Selects new text with limited support Reads familiar and some new easy texts independently Reads new texts with some support (Transitional: Assessment Levels 12–16)
Previewing and Predicting	Gathers limited information about the story from the teacher's introductions and the pictures Comments briefly about each event or action when previewing pictures	Gathers some information about the story from the teacher's introduction and the pictures Begins to connect events when previewing pictures	Gathers pertinent information about the story from the teacher's introduction and the pictures Constructs a tentative story when previewing pictures
Oral Reading and Use of Strategies	Reads word by word Sounds very choppy, stopping at difficulty Relies on support in problem-solving unknown or unexpected known words Detects and corrects miscues with prompting	Generally reads word by word with a few short phrases (2–3 words) Generally sounds choppy, stopping to problem-solve at difficulty Reads with little change in voice, rather monotone Initiates problem-solving of unknown words Detects and self-corrects some miscues	Generally reads in short phrases on the predictable parts of text; some word by word Sounds somewhat choppy with noticeable pauses to problem-s at difficulty Reads with some expression a attention to punctuation; mor at times Uses multiple strategies to problem-solve unknown wor Detects and self-corrects ob miscues
Comprehension	Retelling reflects **very little understanding:** • unorganized • important details missing • incorrect information • misinterpretation	Retelling reflects **some understanding:** • somewhat organized • focuses on parts rather than the whole • events out of sequence • includes some details about characters and events • some misinterpretation • Links to personal experience	

DRA CONTINUUM *K – 3*

EXTENDING READERS

READERS	EXTENDING READERS		
			Book Selection and Sustained Reading
Selects appropriately leveled reading materials most of the time	Selects appropriately leveled reading materials	Selects books for a variety of purposes	
Reads familiar and many new texts independently	Reads most texts independently; new genres with support	Reads texts independently; new genres with some support	
Reads new texts with some support (Transitional: Assessment Levels 18–24)	Reads new texts with minimal support (Extending: Assessment Levels 28–34)	Reads new texts independently (Extending: Assessment Levels 38–44)	
			Previewing and Predicting
Gathers some information from teacher's introduction, paragraphs read aloud, and self-initiated preview	Gathers information from teacher's introduction, paragraphs read aloud, and self-initiated preview	Gathers pertinent information from teacher's introduction, paragraph read aloud, and self-initiated preview	
Makes a prediction	Makes a feasible prediction	Makes multiple predictions	
			Oral Reading and Use of Strategies
Generally reads in longer phrases on the predictable parts of text	Generally reads in longer phrases		
Sounds somewhat smooth with slight pauses at difficulty	Generally sounds smooth; may pause at difficulty	Sounds smooth; may hesitate at difficulty	
Usually reads with expression and attention to punctuation	Reads with effective expression and attention to punctuation	Begins to experiment and explore subtle intonation that reflects mood, pace, and tension	
		Uses strategies automatically	
Uses efficient strategies to problem-solve unknown words	Uses strategies automatically most of the time		
Self-corrects miscues quickly	Makes few miscues		
			Comprehension
Retelling reflects an adequate understanding: • organized but may be choppy • sequential for the most part • includes main ideas, details about characters, settings, and events • literal interpretation	Retelling reflects a very good understanding: • effectively organized and fluid • sequential • includes main idea, important details about characters, setting, and events • reveals use of background knowledge and experience to interpret story • uses vocabulary/special phrases from the story		
Links to other media or events	Links to other literature		

© Upper Arlington City Schools 1996–1997. This DRA form may be copied.

Developmental Reading Assessment Forms

25

BOOK SELECTION
Suggested focus for instruction:

- ✓ Introduce new stories during shared reading and guided reading
- ✓ Introduce and read simple pattern books with child
- ✓ Provide opportunities to select familiar stories for rereading
- ✗ Model how to select new texts for independent reading
- ___ Support and reinforce selection of appropriate reading material
- ___ Introduce new authors
- ___ Introduce new genres
- ___ Introduce book series

SUSTAINED READING
Suggested focus for instruction:

- ✓ Model what to do during sustained reading time
- ___ Support the use of sustained reading time
- ___ Model and support reading with a buddy
- ___ Extend self-sustained reading time
- ___ Support reading familiar as well as new stories at home
- ___ Support involvement in book groups
- ___ Support self-assessment and goal setting

PREVIEWING
Suggested focus for instruction:

- ✓ Model and support creating a story from the illustrations
- ___ Model and support previewing books before reading

PREDICTING
Suggested focus for instruction:

- ___ Model how to predict using title and illustrations
- ___ Model and support predictions of story events and ending during the first reading
- ___ Model and support linking to similar stories
- ___ Model and support use of background knowledge

ORAL READING
Suggested focus for instruction:

- ✓ Encourage joining in on familiar/repeated parts, phrases, and words during read-alouds and shared reading
- ___ Support rereading familiar texts to gain fluency
- ___ Model and support reading in phrases
- ___ Model and support reading dialogues with expression
- ___ Model and support reading longer meaningful phrases with appropriate intonation
- ___ Support reading punctuation

USE OF STRATEGIES
Suggested focus for instruction:

- ___ Model and support moving left to right on text
- ___ Model and support 1 to 1 matching on familiar text
- ___ Demonstrate the concept of first and last, beginning and ending of a word, sentence, story
- ___ Model and support using known words to monitor
- ✓ Model and support using beginning letter(s) and meaning to predict and monitor word choice
- ✗ Model and support confirming and discounting word choice using meaning and visual information
- ✗ Model and support self-detection of miscues
- ___ Support and reinforce self-corrections of miscues
- ___ Model and support using beginning chunks/syllables in words
- ___ Model and support the use of analogies when problem-solving new words
- ___ Reinforce using a variety of strategies to problem-solve new words

COMPREHENSION
Suggested focus for instruction:

- ___ Support and reinforce self-monitoring of meaning across extended text
- ✓ Encourage and support child's responses to books, stories, pictures
- ___ Support discussing stories
- ___ Provide opportunities to discuss characters, sequence of events, problems, and resolutions
- ___ Model possible book extensions
- ___ Support responses to literature through a variety of extensions
- ___ Introduce story mapping
- ___ Provide opportunities to compare/contrast stories, authors, etc.
- ___ Introduce and support literature response journals
- ___ Provide opportunities to analyze and critique stories
- ___ Model and support retelling of familiar stories
- ___ Introduce the elements in a good retelling
- ___ Support effective retellings of stories
- ___ Support word study: compound words, contractions, endings and their meanings
- ___ Extend word study: prefixes, suffixes, root words and their meanings

OTHER
Suggested focus for instruction:

_____
_____
_____
_____

What's Next? Focus for Instruction

After completing the continuum, the teacher uses the "What's Next?" form to determine what the child needs to learn next. This form comprises a checklist of possible interventions in the following categories: book selection, sustained reading, previewing, predicting, oral reading, use of strategies, and comprehension. The teacher can choose from these what next to introduce, model, support, and/or extend.

Using a different pen color to check the focuses for instruction in each grade level helps document the shifts in instruction over time.

Checks reflect observations in kindergarten.

X's reflect observations in first grade.

DRA STUDENT BOOK GRAPH

Name _____

	FALL	SPRING	FALL	SPRING	FALL	SPRING	FALL	SPRING
44 Danger in the Deep								
40 Old Ben Bailey Meets His Match								
38 Trouble at the Beaver Pond								
34 Be Nice to Josephine								
30 Touchdown!								
28 You Don't Look Beautiful to Me								
24 The Wonderful Day								
20 Green Freddie								
18 A Giant in the Forest								
16 The Pot of Gold								
14 The Wagon								
12 Robert's New Friend								
10 Shoe Boxes								
8 Duke								
6 Why Are We Stopping?								
4 Where Is My Hat?								
3 The "I Like" Game								
2 I Can See								
1 Things That Go								
A Can You Sing?								

DRA STAGE:

Grade level / School year	FALL	SPRING	FALL	SPRING	FALL	SPRING	FALL	SPRING
	Emergent	Emergent	Early	Trans.	Trans.	Trans.	Extending	
	Kindergarten 93-94		First Grade 94-95		Second Grade 95-96		Third Grade 96-97	

© Upper Arlington City Schools 1996–1997. This DRA form may be copied.

DRA Student Book Graph

The DRA student book graph represents the increase in level of text difficulty read successfully by the student across his or her primary years. The shaded area on this sample indicates the levels one school district determined to be below proficiency.

DRA Reporting Form

This form may be used by teachers to record students' developmental reading assessment stages and text levels for school or district administrators. If the assessment is used on an annual basis, this form will also enable administrators and teachers to identify students who remain at risk in their development as readers across years.

DRA REPORTING FORM

Building _Barrington_   Teacher _Taps_   Date _'97_

	STUDENT NAMES	DRA STAGE	TEXT LEVEL
		TR	14
1	Chris	TR	24
2	Fred	TR	16
3	Sarah T.	TR	18
4	Amy	TR	18
5	John	TR	20
6	Connie	TR	28
7	Maggie	EX	30
8	J. D.	EX	10
9	Sarah L.	EA	18
10	Sam	TR	18
11	Ray	TR	14
12	Ethan	TR	18
13	Nadia	TR	16
14	Colleen	TR	16
15	Mark	TR	20
16	Jenny	TR	18
17	Marsha	TR	16
18	Sheila	TR	18
19	Natasha	TR	20
20	Oshee	TR	22
21	Brandon		
22			
23			
24			
25			
26			
27			
28			
29			
30			

EM = Emerging   EA = Early   TR = Transitional   EX = Extending

Highlight in yellow those children below proficiency

© Upper Arlington City Schools 1996–1997

School year __96-97__ Teacher __Taps__ Grade level __1__

TEXT READING LEVEL	BEGINNING OF YEAR	END OF YEAR
Emergent A–2	卌 卌 卌	
Early 3–6	卌 /	
8–10	/	
Transitional 12–14	/	
16–18		//
20–24		卌 卌 //
Extending 28		卌
30–34		/
38–40		/
44		
+		
Total #	23	21

Note: __2__ students moved away; ____ students gained during year

DRA Text Levels

If the DRA is administered at the beginning and end of the school year, the DRA text levels form may be used to record the number of students who are reading at the various assessment text levels for a class or school. The information on this form could be helpful to teachers as they consider grouping possibilities for guided reading or small group instruction, or as they celebrate students' growth in text reading levels over the school year. This information could also help administrators to track progress in students' text reading levels, appreciate the progress made, and identify teachers who have greater numbers of challenging or at-risk readers.

PREPARING FOR THE ASSESSMENT

Check to see that you have a complete assessment set.

1

The DRA set includes

- Assessment texts levels A to 44

- An assessment observation guide for each text

- The DRA continuum

- A "What's Next?" focus for instruction form

- A DRA student book graph

- A DRA reporting form

- A DRA text levels form

- A story overview for text levels 4 to 44

Assemble assessment materials.

2

Organize the observation guides, assessment texts, and story overviews by level for easy access and storage. Several possibilities are pocket folders, an expanding file folder, or a notebook. Teachers will need to find what works for them.

Make copies of the assessment forms.

3

For each assessment you will need

- The DRA observation guide for the assessment text you plan to use

- The DRA continuum

- A "What's Next?" focus for instruction form

- The running record form from *An Observation of Early Literacy Achievement* by Marie Clay, pages 25-26. Alternatively, have available a sheet of blank paper on which to take a running record of the student's oral reading.

Keep all original forms in a separate file.

Review or learn how to take a running record.

4

Directions for taking a running record appear in *An Observation of Early Literacy Achievement* by Marie Clay, *Constructive Evaluation of Literate Activity* by Peter Johnson, and *Guided Reading: Good First Teaching for All Children* by Irene Fountas and Gay Su Pinnell.

+ overview for Comprehension

Read all the assessment stories you will be using. familiar

5 ——————

Until the stories become familiar, use the story overviews to help you recall them or to refer to briefly as the student retells. Remember that the overviews are detailed for the teacher's benefit and that primary students should not be expected to retell the story in such detail.

Prepare an assessment time line and activities for the other students.

6 ——————

Generally teachers find they can comfortably assess two children a day. So the assessment window should be set for three to four weeks. Teachers will want to select a time each day for the assessment conferences when other students are engaged in quiet activities that they can self-sustain. While a student reading Level 18 and above reads silently, the teacher may begin another DRA conference or interact with other students.

Prepare students for the DRA.

7 ——————

Prior to the assessment share with students what each will be asked to do during the conference, discuss what the class will do while the teacher is conducting a conference, and describe what makes a good retelling. It would be helpful for students reading assessment levels 8 and above to practice retelling other stories they have read before participating in a DRA conference.

Select and prepare a place for the assessment conference.

8 ——————

The assessment area should be quiet and free from major distractions but allow the teacher to see the rest of the class. Generally, a small table where the teacher can sit beside the child is sufficient. Assessment materials, paper for running records, pen or pencil, and a tape recorder should be within easy reach of the teacher. Audiotaping the student's oral reading permits the teacher to listen a second time for phrasing and fluency if needed.

CONDUCTING THE ASSESSMENT CONFERENCE

Select a beginning level text from the assessment packet.

If the student is obviously an emergent reader, introduce and have the student begin with level A and keep introducing new texts until the student's accuracy rate falls below 90 percent.

If the student is reading beginning-to-mid-first-grade level, select an assessment text you feel the student could read based on your knowledge of his or her performance in guided reading groups or individual reading conferences. Use the locator guide on pages 18–19 to assist you in approximating a child's text level. Introduce the text, have the child tell what is happening in the story while looking through the pictures, and then have the student read the story aloud. If the story is obviously too easy or too difficult, politely stop the reading and then select and introduce another text.

If the student is reading end-of-first-grade level or above, begin with a range of texts from the assessment set that you feel he or she could possibly read. Show the child the selected three or four texts and ask, "Which one do you think would be very easy to read and which one might be too difficult?" From those remaining, ask the student to select the one that seems to be "just right." Read the introductory statement about the story and have him or her read aloud the beginning paragraphs indicated on the observation guide to determine if the text is truly at an appropriate level. If the text seems too difficult or too easy based on the oral reading and prediction, select and introduce another text. Note on the observation guide who selected the text.

Follow the directions on the observation guide for the text selected. Note that the directions do change from level to level. The following are brief overviews of the DRA conferences:

2 ───────

For levels A to 2

Teacher selects the text.

Teacher introduces the text.

Teacher reads one or two pages.

Child points and reads the rest of the story; teacher takes running record.

Teacher asks child to locate a word, letter, etc.

Teacher asks reading preference questions.

For levels 3 to 16

Teacher selects the text.

Teacher introduces the text.

Child looks at the pictures and tells teacher what is happening in the story.

Child reads complete story aloud; teacher takes running record.

Child retells the story.

Teacher asks response questions (e.g., *Did you like this story?*).

Teacher asks reading preference questions (e.g., *Do you like to read?*).

For levels 18 to 44

Teacher selects a range of three texts.

Child chooses one that is just right for him or her.

Teacher introduces the text.

Child reads the first two to four paragraphs aloud.

Child predicts what he or she thinks will happen in the story.

Child reads complete story silently in another location.

Child retells the story.

Teacher asks response questions.

Child reads a selected portion of text aloud; teacher takes running record.

Teacher asks reading preference questions.

In addition for levels 28–44, the teacher asks one or two inference questions.

Record the child's responses and behaviors in the following areas:

3

Previewing and predicting

As a student reading assessment level texts 3 through 16 tells you what is happening in the story based on the illustrations, note if the child begins to construct meaning by gathering pertinent information from the illustrations. Does he or she connect events and begin to construct a story? Are comments disconnected? connected? sounding like a story?

A student reading assessment levels 18 through 44 is asked to predict what he or she thinks might happen in the story after listening to the introductory statement, reading aloud the beginning paragraphs, and possibly flipping quickly through the story. Note if predictions are unlikely, feasible, or multiple.

Oral reading and strategies used

As the student reads aloud, take a running record and note the reader's pace, phrasing, intonation, attention to punctuation, and what happens at difficulty and with miscues. As children become extending readers, processing strategies occur in the head most of the time and are not observable. It may be helpful at first to tape-record the student's oral reading and listen after the DRA conference for phrasing and fluency and to check what the reader does at difficulty. You may want to make a tape for each student to record changes in his or her oral reading over time. Reading strategies are described in Chapter 13, "The Development of Processing Strategies," in *Becoming Literate: The Construction of Inner Control* by Marie Clay, and in Chapter 12 in *Guided Reading: Good First Teaching for All Children* by Irene Fountas and Gay Su Pinnell.

Comprehension

As the student retells the story, check the elements he or she includes. If you prompt the student to tell more, check any added information. Record responses to the specific questions if used and note other questions you asked to discover what else the student remembered about the story. Record an extending reader's responses to the inference questions.

Response

Record the child's responses to the text. Note the level of teacher assistance required by the child in initiating or extending his or her responses.

Reading preferences

Briefly jot down the student's responses to each of the preference questions.

ANALYZING PERFORMANCE

Score and analyze the running record of the oral reading.

1

After completing the DRA conference, determine the student's level of accuracy on the running record by counting the number of miscues and circling the corresponding accuracy rate on the observation guide. (See the sample form on page 21.) Analyze the type of information used by the reader when making and self-correcting miscues. Refer to the three running record resources shown on page 30 for help with analyzing reading behaviors and miscues.

Complete the observation guide.

2

Record the information gained from the running record regarding what the student did at difficulty and with miscues on the oral reading section of the observation guide.

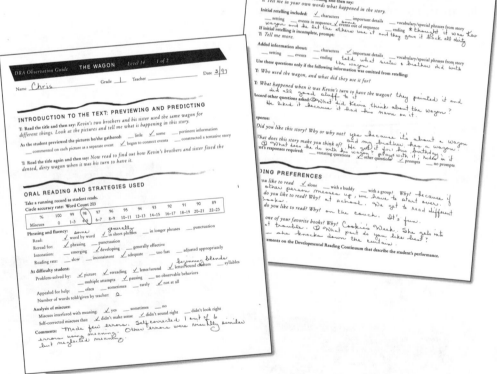

In the comprehension category, to decide which level of understanding best reflects the student's overall understanding of what was read, circle first the statements that describe the student's retelling. Then select one of the following levels of comprehension as a summative statement: very little, some, adequate, or a very good understanding.

Use the designated color for each grade level when circling the descriptors to document changes over time in the student's reading performance. Use purple for kindergartners, red for first graders, green for second graders, and blue for third graders. Refer to the sample continuum on pages 23–25.

Circle the statements on the DRA continuum that best describe the reader's behaviors and responses.

3

A series of statements in four categories on the DRA continuum reflects the range of possible behaviors and responses across the emergent, early, transitional, and extending stages of a reader's development. Read the statements. Then, using the information recorded during the DRA, circle those that best describe the student's behaviors in book selection and self-sustained reading, previewing and predicting, oral reading and use of strategies, and comprehension.

DETERMINING PROFICIENCY

Establish levels of proficiency for your school or district.

Students learn to read and develop as readers at different rates. Using this assessment periodically enables you to monitor changes over time in students' reading performances and confirms ongoing observations and impressions. Some students may need additional literacy instruction and support in learning how to read. Your school or school district will need to establish levels to identify those students who are performing below proficiency. On the student book graph, shade in those levels that they establish to be below proficiency. The following examples of levels of proficiency established by one school district for the fall and spring of each grade level correspond to the book graph on page 27:

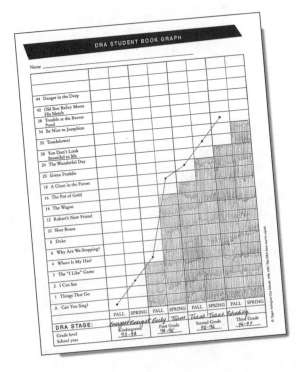

Kindergarten

May/June
Reading levels 1– 2

First Grade

Oct./Nov.
Reading levels 3–6 at 94 percent accuracy or above with some understanding

May/June
Reading levels 16–18 at 94 percent accuracy or above with adequate understanding

Second Grade

Oct./Nov.
Reading levels 18–20 at 94 percent accuracy or above with adequate understanding

May/June
Reading levels 24–28 at 94 percent accuracy or above with adequate understanding

Third Grade

Oct./Nov.
Reading levels 28–30 at 94 percent accuracy or above with adequate understanding

May/June
Reading levels 34–38 at 94 percent accuracy or above with adequate understanding

Identify the children who are performing below proficiency.

2 ⎯⎯⎯⎯

Using the levels selected by the school or district as proficient, identify students who are performing below proficiency. You may keep track of them on the DRA reporting form. See the sample on page 28.

List the students who may need to be reassessed or observed closely to verify DRA observations.

3 ⎯⎯⎯⎯

If a student's comprehension, accuracy rate, or oral reading are less than desired, select a lower-level assessment text and conduct a second DRA conference on another day. (Omit the preference questions this time.) The goal is to find a text level the student can read fairly well and retell adequately. The information gained from a second reading assessment will enable you to decide more effectively what to teach next and how to support this particular reader in his or her text selection and sustained reading time.

A second assessment is especially important for students who are performing below proficiency, even if they qualify for other support services. Teachers must know what levels of text difficulty students are able to read and adequately understand to be able to plan effectively and implement appropriate interventions within the classroom.

✳

If the student is unable to read levels A or 1, have the child try to read

- his or her first name printed on an index card

- his or her first and last names printed on an index card

- names of other family members printed on index cards

- environmental print such as fast-food containers, cereal boxes, and so on

- a very simple caption book that includes objects familiar to the child (a flower, a tree, a cat, a dog, etc.). Demonstrate first and then ask the child to point to the words and read.

Record the student's responses to each task, stopping when he or she is unable to read what is printed. The student's responses will help you know where to begin his or her literacy instruction.

PLANNING YOUR TEACHING

Identify what the child needs to learn next.

1

Students at all levels of proficiency benefit from effective reading instruction. Using the information gained from the child's behaviors observed and responses noted during the DRA, identify what the child needs to learn next. On the "What's Next?" form, place a check by the three or four focuses to introduce, instruct, support, and/or extend. Use the pen color designated for the appropriate grade level. See page 26 for a sample form.

Determine the method of grouping and instructional techniques that will be most effective.

2

After selecting the focuses, you can determine the most effective method of grouping and instructional techniques. The organization of groups will depend on the number of students needing the same type of intervention or reading the same levels. You may choose to introduce, model, or demonstrate for the whole group, a small group, or an individual. Another time you may choose to support and extend effective reading behaviors or strategies through small groups or individual instruction. The number of students that you have indicated on the DRA text level form (see example on page 29) may help determine grouping possibilities.

Keep in mind that when choosing the most effective instruction techniques, it is important to value the reciprocity of the reading and writing processes. Often, especially in the emergent and early stages of reading development, shared and interactive writing can be used for reading instruction. As emergent readers develop early strategies of left-to-right and one-to-one matching, they can benefit from small guided-reading group experiences.

Transitional and extending readers can benefit from literature circles, book groups, and response journals. Other approaches to instruction include reading aloud, shared reading, individual reading and writing conferences, and buddy reading. Independent reading and writing provide students with opportunities to practice and reinforce new learning.

See the other resources at the back of this book for further reading about instructional techniques that are effective when working with primary children.

DOCUMENTING CHANGE OVER TIME

Plot the assessment text level on the student's book graph.

1 ─〰〰〰─

To track the increasing levels of text difficulty read successfully by the student, complete this form as a line or bar graph. Add a dotted line or shading to indicate the levels of proficiency set by your school or district. See page 27 for a completed sample of this graph.

Place the student's DRA continuum with the observation guide and running record in his or her literacy file.

2 ─〰〰〰─

The DRA continuum celebrates and documents a child's reading progress over time and should be kept for future reference along with other records.

SHARING THE RESULTS

Share results and changes over time in a student's reading performance with parents at conferences and in progress reports.

1 ⌇⌇⌇⌇⌇⌇⌇

Sharing a student's DRA continuum and book graph with parents enables them to see and appreciate their child's reading progress across years, especially when the process is begun during kindergarten. The consistent format and language of the continuum fosters parents' appreciation of where their child started and what he or she can do as a reader at the present time. Many of the statements on the continuum may be used on students' progress reports as well.

Share results of the DRA with students when they are able to understand and are beginning to select personal reading goals.

2 ⌇⌇⌇⌇⌇⌇⌇

Sharing their DRA continuums with readers at levels 24 and above enables them to see and appreciate their reading progress across time. The descriptors on the continuum help students to know what is expected of good readers, provide them with the language to discuss and evaluate their performance as readers, and help them to identify possible areas where improvement or extension is needed. This information then enables them to select appropriate personal reading goals and to evaluate their own progress in achieving these goals. Helping these readers to select personal reading goals can be done during a follow-up reading conference.

A Final Word

The DRA may seem overwhelming at first. When you begin to implement it in your classroom, you will have to find an organizational system that works for you. The assessment procedures will begin to feel less cumbersome and easier to do with each assessment you give. After a while, you will know what to do, observe, record on the forms, and circle on the continuum. You will become more adept in describing your observations. Eventually, you will find yourself automatically analyzing students' responses each time you interact with them as readers. Using the information gained from the DRA to select several focuses for instruction will help you to be aware of what individuals or groups of students need to learn, practice, and extend.

It would also help to participate in a training session where videotapes are used to introduce the DRA. Viewing tapes of DRA conferences will help you to see what they are like, understand how the conferences and children's responses vary over time, and discuss with peers how they perceive the various students as readers. Opportunities to discuss observations and perceptions with your peers enable you to confirm your judgments or alter your opinions and establish expectations.

For the sake of time, it may be tempting to shorten the assessment. For example, you may decide just to take a running record, determine a student's accuracy level, and not ask for a retelling or consider how he or she reads orally. If this is the case, remember that accuracy rate is just one factor in determining a student's reading level.

Some students will read a text with a high rate of accuracy and fluency. Others will read rather slowly with a lower rate of accuracy and some phrasing. Even though the first students appear to be the better readers, only the students' retellings will reflect what they understood and recalled about the story.

Reading that is truly satisfying and effective is meaning driven. When students are frequently asked to "read" texts they do not understand, reading becomes a meaningless task that carries little value for them. Therefore, it is important to take the time to listen carefully as students read orally, retell, and respond to the stories read during the assessment and at other times.

It may be just as tempting to decide that a child is an early, transitional, or extending reader because he or she reads a certain assessment text level. However, a child's reading stage can only be truly identified by what his or her reading behaviors and responses reflect. Once again, the text level is just one factor among many. The circled statements help to clarify what each reader does well, where he or she needs support, and what he or she needs to learn next. Knowing these things will help you make more effective teaching decisions and plan more efficiently for ongoing reading instruction.

The DRA has evolved over the years and continues to be revised. As you work with it, you may find places that need further revision so that the forms, continuum, and procedures serve you and your colleagues more efficiently and effectively. Please feel free to send your suggestions and comments to:

Connie Buck
Celebration Press
299 Jefferson Rd., P.O. Box 480
Parsippany, NJ 07054-0480

Your input and feedback will be greatly appreciated.

Joetta Beaver

Other Resources

The DRA was created to assess and document primary students' development as readers over time within a literature-based instructional reading program. A teacher's understanding of early literacy issues, how young children learn, and what they need to learn to read is fundamental. Knowing how to create rich literate environments and learning experiences that honor the way children learn is also essential in establishing an effective early literacy learning program.

Developmentally appropriate assessments are an integral part of the teaching-learning process but cannot stand alone. What happens before and after the assessment is most important. The following articles and books have been found to be useful in furthering teachers' understanding of how to teach children to read and how to support and extend their reading.

Brown, H., and B. Cambourne. 1987. *Read and Retell*. Portsmouth, NH: Heinemann.

Button, K., M. Johnson, and P. Furgerson. 1996. "Interactive Writing in a Primary Classroom." *The Reading Teacher* 49(6):446–454.

Clay, M. M. 1991. "Introducing a New Storybook to Young Readers." *The Reading Teacher* 45:264–73.

Cunningham, P. M., and D. P. Hall. 1994. *Making Words*. Parsippany, NJ: Good Apple Division of Simon and Schuster.

____. 1995. *Phonics They Use*. New York, NY: Harper Collins.

Curriculum Development Branch. 1991. *Reading Resource Book*. Melbourne, Australia: Department of Education of Western Australia.

Department of Education. 1985. *Reading in Junior Classes*. Wellington, NZ: Department of Education.

Huck, C. S., and G. S. Pinnell. 1991. "Literacy in the Classroom." In *Bridges to Literacy: Learning from Reading Recovery*. Edited by D. DeFord, C. Lyons, and G. S. Pinnell, pp. 217–230. Portsmouth, NH: Heinemann.

Lyons, C. A. 1994. "Using Literature to Open the Literate World to Reading Recovery Students: Lessons from Willie." In *Children's Literature in the Classroom: Extending Charlotte's Web*. Edited by J. Hickman, B. Cullinan, and S. Hepler. Norwood, MA: Christopher-Gordon.

McCarrier, A., and I. Patacca. 1994. "Children's Literature: The Focal Point of an Early Literacy Learning Program." In *Children's Literature in the Classroom: Extending Charlotte's Web*. Edited by J. Hickman, B. Cullinan, and S. Hepler. Norwood, MA: Christopher-Gordon.

McKenzie, M. G. 1989. *Extending Literacy: Part One*. Huddersfield, England: Schofield & Sims.

Pinnell, G. S., and A. McCarrier. 1994. "Interactive Writing: A Transition Tool for Assisting Children in Learning to Read and Write." In *Getting Reading Right from the Start: Effective Early Literacy Interventions*. Edited by E. Hiebert and B. Taylor. Needham Heights, MA: Allyn & Bacon.

Schwartz, B. M. Forthcoming. "Self-Monitoring in Beginning Reading." *The Reading Teacher*.

Strong, E. L. 1994. "Creating a Classroom Community for Literature and Literacy." In *Children's Literature in the Classroom: Extending Charlotte's Web*. Edited by J. Hickman, B. Cullinan, and S. Hepler. Norwood, MA: Christopher-Gordon.

Bibliography

Clay, M. M. 1991. *Becoming Literate: The Construction of Inner Control.* Portsmouth, NH: Heinemann.

____. 1993. *An Observation Survey of Early Literacy Achievement.* Portsmouth, NH: Heinemann.

Fountas, I. C., and G. S. Pinnell. 1996. *Guided Reading: Good First Teaching for All Children.* Portsmouth, NH: Heinemann.

Holdaway, D. 1979. *The Foundations of Literacy.* Sydney, Australia: Ashton Scholastic.

____. 1980. *Independence in Reading.* Portsmouth, NH: Heinemann.

Johnston, P. H. 1992. *Constructive Evaluation of Literate Activity.* White Plains, NY: Longman.

Peterson, B. 1991. "Selecting Books for Beginning Readers." *Bridges to Literacy: Learning From Reading Recovery.* Edited by D. DeFord, C. Lyons, and G. S. Pinell. pp 119–147. Portsmouth, NH: Heinemann.

Smith, F. 1986. *Understanding Reading.* Hillsdale, NJ: Erlbaum.

____. 1988. *Joining the Literacy Club.* Portsmouth, NH: Heinemann.